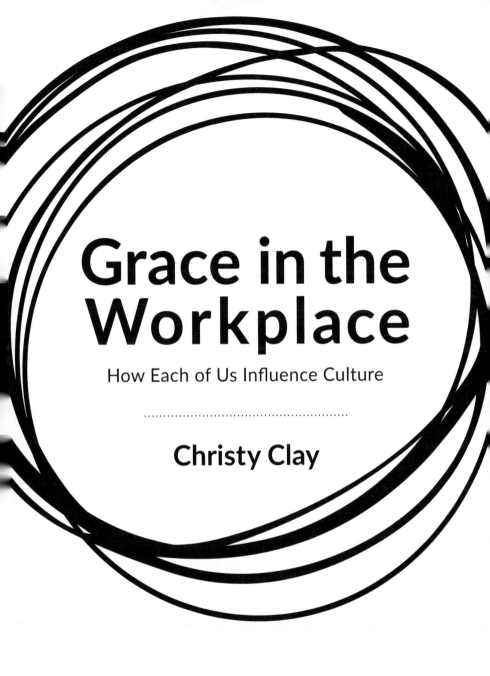

Grace in the Workplace

How Each of Us Influence Culture

Christy Clay

ISBN 9798344127439
Printed by Kindle Direct Publishing
Christy Clay
www.graceintheworkplace.com
christy@graceintheworkplace.com

Dedication

This book is dedicated to my Dad who was smart, wise, and had a heart of gold. When he passed away in 2019, we found this handwritten note in his wallet with these words from Mother Theresa.

People are often unreasonable and self-centered.

<u>Forgive</u> them anyway.

If you are kind, people will accuse you of ulterior motives.

<u>Be kind</u> anyway.

If you are honest, people may cheat you.

<u>Be honest</u> anyway.

If you find happiness, people may be jealous.

<u>Be happy</u> anyway.

The good you do today may be forgotten tomorrow.

<u>Be good</u> anyway.

Give the world the best you have, and it may never be enough.

<u>Give your best</u> anyway.

For you see, in the end, it is between you and God. It was never between you and them - anyway.

Dad, you and your words continue to inspire me. I hope this book makes you proud.

Table of Contents

Introduction

Grace. It's a simple word, yet I have found it to be quite profound and transformational.

Grace has been transformational in that I see the world through a new lens—a clearer, sharper, and softer set of glasses. I discovered that grace sits in direct opposition to judgment (more on this later) and how often I unknowingly judged first, then acted or reacted from this place. Over time, practicing grace interrupted this pattern and invited me to replace judgment with curiosity and thoughtfulness. I became more patient and tolerant of the ways of the world. I saw people's humanity first and their situation or circumstance. I saw this in airports, stores, restaurants—and then in conference rooms. This is where Grace in the Workplace took root.

This book is about my story and the insights and practice that were born from this experience. The practice is simple yet has helped me navigate the complexities of life. The practice is subtle yet can change the quality in which we respond, interact, and connect with others.

This book is a quick read, an efficient dose of wisdom that I hope is as contagious for you as it has been for me. You have likely heard the saying, "We teach what we most need to learn," and there is no exception here. Grace has been a teacher to me, patiently softening my hard edges, bringing me into higher self-awareness, and allowing me to accept the humanness of myself and others. Grace has been a guide and a gift.

My work has been as a business strategist, facilitator, and executive coach for privately-owned businesses and non-profits. Prior to this, I owned and operated several businesses in the recreation, hospitality, and consulting sectors. A central theme throughout my life has been the study of people and understanding why we do what we do. The entirety of my education, undergraduate, graduate, and certifications, have all focused on human and organizational development, leadership, and change. I am certified in DISC and related assessments, all in service to understanding ourselves and our potential.

As a facilitator and coach, I often see the real person behind the leader or managerial role. And what I know from thousands of hours in the trenches, as both participant and observer of the human condition, is that we benefit from a counterbalance to our ego's desire to be right, look good, seek certainty, and maintain control. Our ego offers us motivation, ambition, confidence, and self-identity, among other beneficial attributes. However, unchecked or unbalanced, our ego also limits our ability to listen, collaborate, be creative, and build healthy, productive relationships.

When developing this practice, I was initially hesitant to present grace as a counterbalance or practice in a business context. Would people think it was too "light" or silly? Did I really think grace could make a difference in our workplaces? But the more I shared this premise and practice, the more encouragement I received to spread this message far and wide. My intention for you, reader, is that you will find at least a few "pearls of wisdom" that genuinely improve your life.

I am myself an avid reader. Since my teens, I have been drawn to books and classes that teach me and expand my perspective around people. I often say that I am a lifelong student of the human condition. As you read this book, you will see that I cite many experts in their respective fields, some well-known, others more obscure. In creating the framework and practice of Grace in the Workplace, I referenced these many sources and voices to give it support, credibility, and context. One of my strengths is connecting seemingly unrelated "dots" or concepts and bringing them together to illustrate a fresh perspective that can be of value to others.

This book begins by looking at why grace is at the root of this practice and explaining why it matters. It then gives context to the collective state of our workplaces, followed by our individual roles and responsibilities in that greater context. Then, I share the practice and tools of Grace in the Workplace and how you, the reader, can experiment with it or integrate the parts that resonate with you into your life. It is helpful to read in this order, but it is not necessary. This is not a linear story but more of a reference book—a guide for individuals to understand and practice grace in their respective workplaces.

You will find a blank page prior to Chapter 1. I encourage you to think of a challenging situation or interaction where, in retrospect, you wish you would have responded differently, any interaction at work that left you unsettled. I am not speaking to workplace bullying or harassment; that is outside of my purview and not addressed in this book. I am speaking about a major or minor situation at work that stirred your emotions. If you do not work outside of the home, I encourage you to think of a situation with a friend, child, or partner that you wish you could "do over." The practice of Grace in the Workplace easily applies in all areas of our lives. Take a moment to write this situation or interaction down on this blank page. As you are reading, keep this situation in mind. At the end of the book, I invite you to refer to this situation or interaction and contemplate whether the practice of Grace in the Workplace would have improved it. You be the judge.

I want to thank you for your willingness to explore my story, this subtle but powerful practice, and the role that grace can play in your life. My mission is to inspire Grace in the Workplace—to facilitate improved collaboration, productivity, and well-being through a reduction in workplace incivility and its emotional and financial costs.

Introduction

Chapter 1

Why Grace?

I was on a walk listening to a podcast featuring Richard Rohr, an American Franciscan priest and progressive author. In this podcast, he used the term "transformational wisdom." This phrase resonated deeply with me. Grace, for me, has been *transformational wisdom*.

For context, change is when we learn to do something differently; however, transformation is when we learn to *think and/or act differently*. Our perspective has been shifted, and this shift—or transformation—will impact or change many things over time.

Let me go back to the beginning. This journey to grace started for me as a personal, albeit very casual, assignment that had no association with grace. For years, I had been witnessing someone close to me being rude and impatient with those working on the "front lines" of life, people working as cashiers or in customer service, often in demanding and thankless jobs. It was uncomfortable to watch and ultimately bothered me enough to make a conscious and concerted effort to be just the opposite. As a counterbalance, I would be thoughtful and patient, and I did so for enough years that it became habitual. Years later, this same person who inspired me initially commented, "Christy, you are always so kind to people at stores and restaurants." As I thought about this comment, I had a significant realization. I realized that although my intention was to be thoughtful and giving to others, over time, I had directly benefited as well. I would walk away from these interactions with people I didn't know and feel lifted up. I connected with a stranger, we had shared a nice exchange and sometimes a brief laugh. My effort to brighten their day, if only for a moment, had brightened mine too. Why was that? I took some time to reflect on this and found myself smack in the middle of the tenet: *it is better to give than to receive*. That is when I recognized that this was grace.

Grace was not a word I used or thought about much, yet it came forth with stunning clarity. Why the word grace, and what does it mean exactly? The formal definition I found most fitting in my experience was "favor or goodwill; benevolence". As I explored the concept of grace, I found that it encourages us to see our commonality and our humanness in one another. It allows us to extend compassion and kindness to ourselves and others. Grace is both a secular and sacred word. It applies to those who have no spiritual or religious beliefs. And for those who do, they may describe it as the free and unmerited favor of God.

Either way, the true beauty of grace is that it is unmerited. We simply give or receive kindness, favor, goodwill, or forgiveness. We do not need to earn grace; it is offered or extended without strings or expectations. It is the best of us as humans.

As I was beginning to understand and appreciate grace, it occurred to me that in the performance and merit-based culture we live in today, grace can seem counterintuitive—almost foreign and out of touch with our hustle culture. We operate more in a world of quid pro quo. Much of our lives require this exchange; certainly, at work, we are compensated for fulfilling specific roles. But when life is too heavily focused on quid pro quo and performance, it can feel unbalanced.

Grace is a welcome counterbalance. It has been present for thousands of years through many divisive periods in our history. From a historical perspective, I think of examples during wartime, slavery, and natural disasters.

At the end of WWII, Japanese pilot Hideichi Kaiho had "downed" a bomber over Tokyo, forcing the American crew to bail from the aircraft. Moments later, Kaiho and two other Japanese planes spotted these men—their enemies—in parachutes. Miraculously, two planes simply flew away, and Kaiho continued to fly around them for protection. Five decades later, an American named Raymond Holloran would meet Kaiho in person to thank him for saving his life that day. Kaiho responded that he was observing the "Bushido code," which espoused graciousness towards the enemy.

The Underground Railroad was grace—and courage—personified. Born into slavery in Maryland in 1822, Harriet Tubman was beaten and whipped by her enslavers. Escaping in 1849 to Philadelphia, Tubman continued to go back to Maryland to free others. She traveled with these newly escaped people during the night and in extreme secrecy, depending on the kindness and grace of freed Black people, white abolitionists, and other activists. She ultimately freed seventy people and "never lost a passenger."

In the book *A Paradise Built in Hell*, Rebecca Solnit writes about the disastrous earthquake and subsequent fires that left three thousand dead and half of

San Fransisco residents homeless. She describes a woman named Anna Amelia Holshouser, who was forced to camp out with a friend, eventually setting up in Golden Gate Park. Holshouser made a makeshift tent out of fabric scraps that provided shelter for twenty-two people and started a tiny soup kitchen that grew to feed two hundred to three hundred daily.

These dire circumstances illustrate that grace is available for us anytime we are willing to give it or receive it. Yet, in our complex, fast-paced, and distracted culture, it can be in that very simplicity that we underestimate its transformative power.

As I continued to ponder what this transformative power was for me and why I was receiving more than I was giving, it finally became clear. Grace was a pathway to more consistent personal integrity.

Personal integrity is when we operate as or embody the person we aspire to be, the identity we associate with ourselves. I aspire to be kind, thoughtful, caring, and respectful. I want to be someone who would give people the benefit of the doubt. And I often behaved that way when it was easy, when things went as I anticipated or expected. But I did not always behave that way when things were adverse, difficult, or not on my timeline.

Practicing grace in this one area of my life taught me that behaving as the person I aspire to be is energy-giving, life-affirming. It strengthened my ability and resolve to do so in other areas of my life. It was at this time that I started to think about applying this practice to the workplace. As a consultant and facilitator, I had seen team infighting, posturing, egoic behavior, and more—almost always from genuinely good people. Could grace inspire others in the way it inspired me? Could grace be a pathway to personal integrity—to increased civility, respect, and teamwork—in the workplace? The seed was planted.

I did research to see where and how this could apply and drew on the experiences of myself and others. I found a body of research on workplace incivility that I will expound on in Chapter 2. I found Harvard Business School articles on the power of curiosity. I found high-profile CEOs talking about compassionate leadership. I gathered, listened, learned, and analyzed. I shared this concept and the practice with clients and friends. CEOs of multi-million-dollar businesses leaned in and said, "Tell me more." Some leaders said little initially yet circled back later with comments like, "Yeah, I get it now" or "I wasn't exactly sure what I thought when I read your work, but I cannot unhear it, and it has altered how I respond, how I hold myself accountable."

And although the word grace falls outside of our workplace vernacular, I knew it was the right word. I then discovered a book by tech executive and prolific best-selling author Seth Godin, entitled *Graceful: Making a Difference in a World that Needs You, in which he writes,* "The thing is that no one is born graceful. It's not a gift, it's a choice."

From here, I was inspired and determined to create the practice of Grace in the Workplace as an invitation to anyone who is open to exploring it. Grace had quite simply transformed my worldview over time. I'd shifted from a largely unconscious lens of judgment to a lens of genuine curiosity towards others. I discovered that being patient and compassionate with others left me feeling better, calmer and stronger. Grace created connection.

It is estimated that we spend about 70 to 80 percent of our waking hours engaged in some form of interpersonal communication and I believe that Grace in the Workplace can offer a welcome levity to the complexity of emotions that can at times surround our communications.

Now that you're familiar with the concept of Grace in the Workplace and how it can help us to lead more fulfilled, enriching, and community-oriented lives, let's explore the antagonist of grace: incivility.

Chapter 2

The Rise in Incivility

A nationwide survey entitled "Civility in America" quantified that 70 percent of Americans believed incivility had reached "crisis proportions." Although this statistic is not unique to workplaces, I believe this plays out at work in similar proportions, if not higher, due to the competitive nature of work.

What is workplace incivility? It is commonly described as disrespect or rudeness. It can be subtle, as in our tone (verbal or electronic), negative assumptions, lack of support, or interrupting or excluding people. It can be more obvious, such as teasing, using insults or offensive jokes, or disregarding someone.

As the communicator or sender, we often assume that we determine if we have been uncivil, but it is the receiver who determines this. As individuals, we have different tolerances, experiences, preferences, and sensitivities. Most people experience and contribute to workplace incivility, albeit in varying degrees.

The body of research on workplace incivility conducted by Christine Porath and Christine Pearson is featured in the *Harvard Business Review* article entitled "The Price of Incivility." They articulate the prevalence of incivility, why incivility matters, and its financial impacts.

The prevalence is as follows:

- 85 percent of employees deal with conflict on some level
- 29 percent of employees deal with it almost constantly
- 30-43 percent of managerial time is spent mediating conflict between employees
- More than 65 percent of performance problems result from strained relationships between employees

For those who experience workplace incivility, the research found the following:

- 48 percent intentionally decreased their work effort
- 47 percent intentionally decreased their time at work
- 38 percent intentionally decreased the quality of their work
- 80 percent lost work time worrying about the incident
- 66 percent said their performance declined
- 78 percent said their commitment to the organization declined
- 25 percent admitted to taking their hostility out on customers

Based on this body of research, Cisco estimated that workplace incivility conservatively cost them $12M each year. The researchers Pearson & Porath quantify it as $14,000 per employee per year due to lost productivity and work distraction. Other research by

Patricia Lewis & Ann Malecha quantified the cost of workplace incivility at around $11,500 per employee.

More examples of workplace incivility are an undermining or disparaging comment made in a meeting or public forum, taking credit for other's efforts, passing blame for our own mistakes, spreading rumors about colleagues, talking down to others, not listening, belittling other's efforts, snippy emails, checking email or texting during a meeting, consistently interrupting or talking over a co-worker, gossiping, withholding information, showing little interest in others' opinions, or dominating conversations to exert control. Most of us have found ourselves on both sides of incivility.

Before I address why this matters, let's take a look at how we got here. We say "business isn't personal," but it is. We've moved from the industrial revolution, a largely factory system that embodied mass production and minimal creativity, to the knowledge economy, where our individual knowledge, skills, creativity, and collaboration are vital. We are asked to bring our ideas to the table, to adapt, innovate, grow, and develop.

This is why work is personal. Leah Weiss, in her book *How We Work: Live Your Purpose, Reclaim Your Sanity & Embrace the Daily Grind*, claims, "Partly because work is where we spend so much of our time and partly because of its nature, nothing provides more opportunities than the workplace for us to feel discouraged, disappointed, bored, overwhelmed, envious, embarrassed, anxious, irritated, outraged and afraid to say what we really feel."

This isn't bad or good, right or wrong; it is simply the human condition. And because our work is personal today, Weiss says, "We all want our work to matter, and we all want to matter to our work."

And there has been a shift in our culture over the past several decades. You may have experienced it trying to get assistance at a store, driving on the interstate, reading an email from a co-worker, or having a political conversation with a neighbor. There are countless examples. The academics who have researched this refer to it as incivility.

In addition, our pace has changed in the past several decades, along with our often-unconscious relationship with— or, at times, addiction to—busyness. It has incrementally accelerated year over year, fueled by technology and global competitiveness. Today, Americans work more hours and take less vacation time; this decreased margin affects our coping skills. Our smartphones allow us to check our email when we wake up in the middle of the night. This increased pace and pressure play out in countless ways: road rage, our general health (is anyone not tired?!), the rise of autoimmune diseases, the sharp increase in anxiety and depression—and everyday incivility.

Busy is the current zeitgeist but not our only option. There is a strong body of evidence on the ineffectiveness of chronic busyness detailed in the best-selling books Essentialism by Greg McKeown, The One Thing by Gary Keller and Jay Papasan, and *Deep Work* by Cal Newport.

At a high level, the general landscape of our professional lives is impacted by:

- The Human Condition: The nature of our work environments will trigger emotions.
- Increased Pace: Reduced time affects our coping skills and patience.
- Knowledge Worker: The pressure to perform, create, innovate, and prove our worth.
- Scarcity Mindset: Operating from threat vs. trust; threat suggests there isn't enough time, money, customers, profit, etc., causing us to strive and hustle more.
- Communication Through Technology: Words can easily be misinterpreted in the absence of visual and tonal cues.

These are certainly not all the factors, but they are key factors in the significant statistics around workplace culture and incivility. Experts claim that of all the harmful workplace behaviors covered in their research, **incivility is the most low-key yet chronic and ubiquitous form**. It points to incivility being prompted by thoughtlessness rather than malice. I know this has certainly been the case for me.

Have you ever had what I call an "incivility hangover"? This is where you later thought, why did I respond that way? I could have been kinder, patient, inquisitive, and/or listened more—any number of attributes. I call it a hangover because it lingers. I don't feel settled about my response or reaction even when I move on and pretend it doesn't bother me; when I tell myself, *I mean, let's face it, they were in the wrong.* The way I responded nests inside of me and creates unease.

What the heck does this all have to do with grace?

Well, because our work is personal, and because *who* we are at work and *how* we behave as contributors can be as important to our career success as *what* we do, it all matters. It all impacts performance—and performance impacts results and profits.

If I look back at my own experiences, despite clear intentions to be a mature, thoughtful contributor, at times when I was faced with uncomfortable emotions or stress, I responded quickly and unconsciously, adding to the very workplace dysfunction I wished in earnest would change.

Yet this honest revelation also brought me to another significant discovery. I had always believed that I was not a part of the workplace drama, I was one of the "good guys." I believed that this was happening to me, not *with* me, right?

What I was failing to appreciate at the time was my own power, the role I played in perpetuating workplace incivility vs. practicing grace. To learn how not to contribute to workplace dysfunction, I would have to understand a key factor of Grace in the Workplace and the focus of our following chapter—*agency*.

Chapter 3

Our Agency

One thing I find utterly fascinating is that during natural disasters like a hurricane, fire, or tornado, or a man-made disaster like 9/11, people go to impressive lengths to show up for strangers and exude and embody magnificent grace. People pick up at a moment's notice and drive across state lines to help strangers. They put aside political, racial, and religious differences and lend help. Why? What about disasters or crises makes this so instinctual for us? And conversely, what about an election can make it so difficult to extend grace?

The answer involves collective factors as well as factors that are unique to each person. In great generality, a crisis can be an equalizer and often facilitates service over ego. The urgency of a disaster helps us to suspend our mental constructs and respond with our most primal emotions.

Why is it so easy to exhibit grace in the face of a big crisis and often so difficult with our smaller, everyday interactions? What can these situations teach us about our everyday interactions?

It is a virtually universal preference to work for a company with a positive culture. This is captured in the well-known quote by Peter Drucker: "Culture eats strategy for breakfast." In this, Drucker suggests that culture permeates more than strategy. For years, in my mind, workplace culture, incivility, and its close cousins—dysfunction, toxicity, gossip—whatever you choose to call it—all seemed to be happening outside of, or to me, as if I was not an active participant in shaping culture. But through the lens of grace, I came to recognize that I am a part of the workplace drama; that the drama is happening *with* me.

To illustrate this, I will share an example from my own experience. I was a director at an organization that I loved working for, and at times, I was frustrated with my boss. When in this situation, I would go to a co-worker's office to "vent" about what was, in my opinion, an unreasonable request. There were other times I was upset about a passive-aggressive or confusing comment he had made. In my discomfort, I would again respond by choosing to go into my co-worker's office to talk about how our mutual boss "should" be behaving differently (because I am clearly under the illusion that I know better). When I made this choice, I have now become a part of the very dysfunction I complain about. I am contributing to the culture, the environment, and not in a positive or healthy way.

With the clarity of hindsight, I see that this is straight-up gossiping. I am taking a problem to someone, a co-worker, who cannot be a part of the solution. She was likely focused on her work, and I interrupted her and likely stirred her emotions as well. And if I'm being honest, for years, I felt justified in this type of behavior because, after all, hadn't I been wronged?! Hadn't he been in the wrong in treating me this way?

I felt justified because I was only seeing it through the lens of what I perceived was happening to me. But the truth is that my venting created an environment of negativity and judgment and interrupted workflow. It was purely an egoic action for me to feel better, to cajole a colleague to affirm and confirm how right I was.

But did I improve or solve anything? I did not. Did I act with personal integrity? I did not. Not only that, but I also created tension and unwelcome emotions that were unnecessary. It was immature and certainly not graceful—I exhibited no curiosity or goodwill for my boss as a person.

Did I pause to think of the pressure and stress my boss may have been under?

Did I consider that he may have had some frustrations with me or my work?

Did I talk with him directly about my concerns or feelings about our interactions?

Did I offer him the benefit of the doubt—or goodwill—knowing he works hard, too?

I did not.

And what I have come to realize is that we are all a part of this. With few exceptions, we are all adding to what I call the "metaphorical fire." This is what I mean by personal agency: that each of us understands that we influence, cause, or generate our own circumstances. Not 100 percent, but we often have more agency in these situations than we acknowledge. Culture is happening *with* us, not to us.

I finally recognized that I was adding embers to this fire of incivility, minor dysfunction, and toxic behavior. Some days, it was a small ember, sometimes a stick or a log, but rest assured, I had my role, and I suspect you have had your role at times, too.

The actions in my example were unproductive and unkind. They promoted gossip, negativity, and dysfunction. Is this the kind of leader or co-worker I was? Not always, not most days, but on some days, I was. And the short-term release of my emotions had a trailing effect I was not considering. I believe this is important to talk about because, without our awareness, we will continue feeling justified in our gossip and our negativity. **But the truth is we are continuing as a part of the problem versus a part of the solution.**

With this insight that culture and workplace drama happen with us, I believe it is beneficial to look at our personal agency, our part or responsibility in shaping the collective culture and our environment at work. Workplace culture, largely defined as the personality of an organization, significantly impacts both employee productivity and retention.

Finding yourself within the workplace incivility statistics shared in Chapter 2 can elicit any number of unwelcome emotions. We internalize and carry these emotions around. We talk about workplace dysfunction in hushed tones at work; we talk about it to our family and friends outside of work. A colleague sent an accusatory email, was undermining, responded inappropriately, or didn't acknowledge our part in an important project. Our boss or co-worker is irritating or frustrating us, is undermining us, they don't know what they are doing, they don't have our back...the list goes on. I imagine you can pull several examples from your own experience. In my experience, and for many of those that I have coached, we describe this as happening *to* us—that it is someone else's fault; they are creating it.

But the breakthrough here is that we are inside of this equation—and shaping culture is our role, too, not just that of leadership. It is both individual and collective. Culture is shaped both from the top down and the bottom up. We don't have to wait for leadership or anybody else to change. And once we have this aware-ness, once we know better, we can do better. We can get clear on the person we aspire to be and operate within our personal integrity.

Each one of us, as individuals, is a part of this solution. **We have 100 percent agency in how we show up, how we react and respond, even when the going gets tough**, even when we feel like people have wronged us. Despite being a small slice by percentage, our decisions and how each one of us chooses to behave adds up collectively and will have an impact across an organization.

I encourage us all to bring self-awareness and full responsibility for how we handle the impact and influ-ence we do have. Ideally, company culture is set at the top, and the leaders live it, but this does not absolve us of our personal contribution. How are you showing up? How are you doing your part?

The good news is that not everyone has to practice workplace grace for it to have a widespread effect on company culture. In his book Change: *How to Make*

Great Things Happen, Damon Centola suggests that a tipping point of merely 25 percent is required to start a cascade effect that can bring about considerable change. Centola's 25 percent tipping point theory says that when a quarter of a group agrees with a certain point of view or acts in a certain way, it can become the new norm. This is also demonstrated in Malcom Gladwell's best seller *The Tipping Point* in what he refers to as "the law of the few". We don't need everybody; just one in four can create a positive and collective impact.

It can feel normal and productive to focus on others and how they may improve or do it differently. It all seems so clear when we look at others. But what is most important and impactful is if we all take responsibility for ourselves and focus on our agency and our personal integrity.

With that, it is time to introduce the practice of Grace in the Workplace, or what I profess to be "culture change by the people, for the people."

Chapter 4

The Practice of Grace in the Workplace

We have looked at the current culture, our environment, and our own role in shaping culture. Now it is time to share the framework for Grace in the Workplace. It encompasses four attributes: compassion, kindness, curiosity, and goodwill. This chapter will examine each attribute individually as well as how they work together.

Grace is COMPASSION

In this framework, compassion is the foundation, the bedrock for Grace in the Workplace, because it provides perspective—an expanded lens and worldview.

Our culture of busyness leads us to a more myopic perspective. Our heads are so full of our own "stuff"—work, family, bills, illness, repairs, relationships, whatever may be occupying or challenging us—that we often don't take the time or energy to really see each other. Yes, we exchange pleasantries, share pictures on social media, and talk about the weather or news headlines, but do we engage long enough, or deep enough, to really learn about what others are facing? In the context of work, we may not know specifics, but we can bring a general understanding that all of us face challenges.

I will speak about compassion from both a personal and professional perspective. You have likely seen or heard the quote, "Be kind, for everyone you meet is fighting a battle you may know nothing about." This is the personal perspective on compassion. Compassion is our ability to recognize that despite how someone may look or be functioning, we likely do not know their whole story or situation. The human condition involves discomfort, pain, and suffering for all, obviously to varying degrees. We go through and grow through different phases of life. Sometimes, pain is clear and evident, and other times, it is masked by expensive clothing or impressive titles, meaning we can fall into the assumption that favorable financial circumstances preclude people from the trials of life.

The truth is we simply don't know what is going on with most of the people we cross paths with, sometimes even those we know well. Brené Brown, an author and researcher, illustrates this point when she says, "Everyone has a story or a struggle that will break your heart. And if we're really paying attention, most people have a story that will bring us to our knees." We don't need to know one another's stories to have compassion. We simply need the perspective that no one escapes the peaks and valleys, the ebb and flow, and the trials and blessings of the human condition.

Peter Frost, an early and influential leader on compassion in the workplace, said, "There is always pain in the room." Our co-workers, colleagues, bosses, and leaders may be struggling with any number of issues that we know nothing about, and this general awareness can help us to extend compassion. We've all been "there" or will be there at some time in our career, that person with pain in the room. Some of us will mask it or handle it well, yet we all have the capacity for it to play out "sideways." By this, I mean we may express it in an illogical way, such as a customer issue, a curt email, an off-color comment, a harsh response, or unwarranted feedback. It is not uncommon for us to take our internal discomfort or strife and express it in unproductive ways at work. When someone is reacting or behaving in a manner that is unusual for them, this is likely at play. In these instances, compassion and grace provide support that we may not have the wherewithal to ask for but that we all need at some time in our work lives.

We don't know what is happening in the totality of other people's lives. Despite this, can we respond through the lens of compassion?

In 2016, Glassdoor did a survey of CEOs in the United States, and Jeff Weiner, CEO of LinkedIn at that time, received the highest rating of 100 percent approval. When interviewed about this, he directly attributed his success to leading compassionately, which has been his focus for over a decade.

Prior to this, in the early 2000s, a journalist described Jeff Weiner's management style at Yahoo as "wielding his fierce intelligence as a blunt instrument." His response to this comment was something to the effect of, "At least the first part was flattering." At that time, Mr. Weiner admits that although he wasn't a yeller, he was pretty intense. If something in a presentation didn't make sense, he might barrage the team with questions. He would listen to his team, not with the intent to listen or seek to understand but to formulate his reply. He expected other people to do things the way he did and grew frustrated when they didn't. He recognized that rather than inspiring and lifting people up, this style was mostly a way to shut people down.

So he challenged himself to change, and through a couple of personal situations and mentors, he aspired to manage compassionately. This meant, in his words, "pausing and being a spectator...especially when getting emotional. It meant walking a mile in the other person's shoes and understanding their hopes, their fears, their strengths, and their weaknesses. And it meant doing everything to set them up to be successful." After practicing this approach for well over a decade, he claims with absolute conviction that managing compassionately is not just a better way to build a team; it's a better way to build a company.

When I coach executives and professionals one-on-one, I conduct an initial interview and have the client complete a questionnaire designed to identify and capture where they are today and what they envision and desire for their future. My job as a coach is then to read between the lines and extract limiting beliefs, old narratives, or subconscious blocks that may be holding them back. I was working with a client in her mid-thirties who had spent ten years excelling in both position and influence, as well as financially. She had experienced more career success than she had ever envisioned. As we commenced our coaching relationship, she was overwhelmed with work and life, yet ambitious to keep advancing her career.

I was able to identify a lack of self-compassion as one of the primary sources of her feeling overwhelmed. She had been using stress as a motivator and had unconsciously found comfort in chaos. As I reflected this to her, I suggested she may benefit from bringing compassion and self-awareness to this adaptive strategy. Yes, stress can be an effective motivator—and is, at times, the reality of our work lives—but it will exhaust and deplete us over time. The origins of stress are rooted in fear and scarcity and will ultimately limit us. Her ability to recognize this and, over time, replace stress with vision and impact as motivation was born from a place of compassion.

The situation with this coaching client is not unique. From ambitious CEOs to younger developing leaders, self-awareness and compassion almost always play a critical role in accessing greater potential—Jeff Weiner described this for himself. As a coach, this is not something I advertise or overtly talk about because most of my clients believe they simply need to figure out how to "do or be better." If I told them upfront that compassion may be a key element, they would likely assume I don't know what I am doing, yet time and time again, it has been a primary lever in moving professionals toward their desired future.

Compassion widens our myopic lens. It is a stance of expansion that opens us up to improved interactions and greater well-being. How do we practice or extend compassion to others? We think before we act, react, or respond. As Jeff Weiner states, "We walk a mile in the other person's shoes." We understand that some days being human is just plain more difficult than others. We think about and care for the greater good of others. Below is a sampling of questions to guide compassion.

Did I think about their perspective, where they may be coming from?

Did I consider that this person may be having a tough day, week, month, or year?

Did I consider that this person's tone and/or interaction with me may have nothing to do with me?

Did I remember that this person, like me, has fears, weaknesses, and insecurities?

Did I realize that fear may be driving their communications? If so, can I be compassionate about this?

Grace is KINDNESS

Did you know that kindness—the simple, been-around-forever-it-can-almost-seem-boring-kindness— has been proven to reduce stress, anxiety, depression, and pain, as well as leave you feeling calmer, healthier, and happier?

It has been established that if you perform just one random act of kindness a day, you will receive the benefits listed above. Additionally, kindness is about the only thing in the world that doubles when you share it. When you extend kindness to others, both you and the recipient of your kindness experience these benefits. Kindness is more powerful than many modern medicines, and in this case, the prescription is free and organic. This research is provided by the Random Acts of Kindness Foundation in a video they produced entitled *The Science of Kindness*. You can easily find it on the Internet.

Kindness is teachable and contagious. We all have the capacity to extend kindness, but how often is it at the top of our minds at work? One of the most important messages from *The Science of Kindness* video is that "it all starts with just one person, you!" Each one of us, individually, can choose kindness, and when we do, its contagion has the potential to spread far and wide.

As I have matured and witnessed people being unkind, I wonder where they learned this and how unkind they are to themselves. Or how unaware or unconscious they are of how they are treating others. Sometimes, being unkind is just situational, a bad day, or a high-stress level that results in a random act of indifference or unkindness. If this is the case, I suggest we offer this person grace. We have all experienced this.

Sometimes, it is not a bad day, but a bad habit—a way of operating, a defense mechanism—that was likely learned in formative years or through a tough life experience. If this is the case, how amazing is it that we have the power to respond with kindness and not make things worse? I know, I know, we often think if someone is rude, insensitive, or indifferent to us, we are justified in being rude, insensitive, or indifferent in return. A tit for a tat, an eye for an eye, right? Or we can rise above and choose kindness as a salve, a medicine. It is all within our control; it is all our choice. Kindness is healthy, teachable, and contagious.

A former CEO of Campbell's Soup, Doug Conant, credits kindness for allowing him to turn the business side of things around. Hired in 2001, Campbell's Soup was at an organizational low point. Their market share had dropped in half, sales were declining, and people were being laid off. Mr. Conant was hired to turn things around, and he did. It took him five years to "right the ship," and within nine years, they were winning awards, including Best Places to Work. He did this by having (in his words) high standards, but also—and most importantly—encouraged everyone, including himself, to do it with civility. He described civility as "tough-minded on standards and tender-hearted with people." He encouraged all leaders to recognize "daily touch points" with their staff as an opportunity to make them feel valued—to be agile and mindful for these times when they could use civility to lift their staff up. Mr. Conant personally wrote over thirty thousand thank you notes to employees while at Campbell's Soup. For more than a decade, he has been preaching the benefits of kindness, among other things, as a successful leadership consultant.

James Rhee is another excellent example of using kindness to propel the success of organizations he works with. Rhee is a high school teacher and Harvard Law graduate who became a private equity investor and then a CEO. His experience led him to "bridge math with emotions by marrying capital with purpose." In his book *red helicopter—a parable for our times: lead change with kindness (plus a little math)*, he writes, "Creating a culture of kindness at work distributes the joy of problem-solving to everyone, creates a safe environment that unleashes innovation, and turns perceived liabilities into assets to create real equity value in every meaning of the word."

These examples demonstrate that kindness is not just found in platitudes; kindness creates real value and connection in our workplaces. I recognize that kindness is more akin to a schoolyard playground than a corporate boardroom, yet it holds power and deserves our attention and intention in our workplaces. Let's leverage the influence, medicinal properties, and contagion of kindness for greater well-being at work.

We've all experienced how kindness can lift our spirits and change our mood or mindset on a dime. And we've also experienced the opposite. In this way, each of us has the capacity to be a change agent for good. Below are questions on intentionally choosing kindness at work.

Can I respond with kindness regardless of how others are behaving? If others are being unkind or immature, responding with like energy often amplifies the negative.

Did I remember that kindness is contagious and encouraging to others?

Did I remember that extending kindness can help my stress level—along with those I am kind to?

How could kindness or generosity improve this interaction or situation?

Grace is CURIOSITY

I will begin and end this attribute with what I believe to be true...that curiosity is the new confidence. When I initially share the practice of Grace in the Workplace with others, I get the most questions about curiosity; it seems unexpected, a bit out of place. Yet, not unlike compassion, curiosity opens our minds and widens our perspective, which is all a part of extending or practicing grace.

I was born naturally curious and have always asked a lot of questions. I genuinely enjoy learning and hearing others' perspectives and have said countless times that I believe beauty is in the blend of perspectives—meaning ideas, solutions, and the like, are often strengthened by multiple viewpoints and collaboration. A recent Harvard Business Review article entitled *The Business Case for Curiosity* cites that just the act or practice of curiosity caused people to work together more effectively, reduced conflict, and improved both team performance and results. I don't know of any business or organization that is not seeking these very outcomes.

Exploring curiosity led me to also explore the opposite of curiosity, which is certainty. I examined when real or perceived certainty closed me off to curiosity—and it was far more than I care to admit. When I was trying to look smart, prove competencies, or maintain the illusion of control, I had (mostly) blocked out curiosity. To become more conscious of this, I developed a tool, which I now share with clients. It is a very simple spectrum with curiosity at one end and certainty at the opposite end, helping me, and now helping us, gauge where we are.

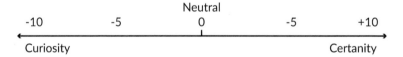

I use this visual to bring heightened self-awareness to my level of curiosity. I assess where I find myself on the spectrum in the present moment and if this aligns with where I aspire to be. Often, the very nature of our professional work is to get to higher levels of certainty and remove as much uncertainty as possible. Many professions rely on certainty—surgeons, engineers, air traffic controllers, worksite safety—you get the idea. I will refer to this as productive certainty—repeatable certainty that ensures favorable results.

But for now, I will speak about unproductive certainty, the certainty that comes from a closed mindset, ego, our need to prove, and our desire to be right. The certainty that feels synonymous with confidence. I know I have found unproductive comfort in this type of certainty.

Brené Brown, who works with successful leaders on vulnerability and courage, calls it armored leadership vs. daring leadership. Armored leadership is characterized by being a "knower" and needing to be right. Daring leadership is characterized by being a learner, being curious, and being open as we try to "get it right" with the input of others.

Our culture has historically lauded "knowers." Yet even in our "knowing professions," we continue to learn and apply continuous improvement. Surgeons improve the process and their technique; engineers apply new technologies to improve the process, precision, and outcome. If we look back one hundred years, even twenty years, we can see that nothing is known and stagnant forever. Our scientific fields and evidence continue to evolve and expand. Think quantum physics, epigenetics, neuroscience, food and nutritional science, and medical technologies, to name a few. All of the advances in these fields involved curiosity, and the best minds in the best workplaces recognize this.

The research claims that armored leadership, or needing to know everything, is miserable for the "knowers" themselves and for everyone around them. A fixed mindset is limiting. The big shift here is from needing to "be right" to wanting to "get it right." How can curiosity serve us here?

Satya Nadella became the new CEO of Microsoft in 2014, and soon after, he asked the company's top executives to read a book by Marshall Rosenberg called *Nonviolent Communication*, which focuses on empathic collaboration. This gesture signaled that Nadella planned to run the company differently from his well-known predecessors, Bill Gates and Steve Ballmer, both of whom ran it in a hierarchical and more dominant manner. This book and what Nadella called a partnership-centered approach addressed Microsoft's long-standing reputation as a "hive of intense corporate infighting".

Today, Nadella credits this book for helping to reshape the culture. He has inspired the company's 124,000 employees to embrace what he calls "learn-it-all" curiosity over what he describes as Microsoft's historical "know-it-all" bent. This, in turn, has inspired developers and customers—and investors—to engage with the company in new, more modern ways.

Nadella had the courage to emphasize the soft skills that are often minimized in the cutthroat world of corporate politics and technology yet essential in today's marketplace to facilitate performance. And the results have been remarkable. Under Nadella's leadership, not only has Microsoft been restored to relevance, but the company also generated more than $250 billion in market value in just three and a half years—more value growth over that time than Uber and Airbnb, Netflix and Spotify, Snapchat and WeWork. In fact, as this was cited in 2018, more than all those companies combined. Yes, there were many factors that contributed to this, but it also demonstrates the power of curiosity.

How often do you draw on your curiosity? Do you think curiosity could help you in collaborating with others? To judge others less? How does it serve us to be more curious than certain? I come full circle here back to my belief that "curiosity is the new confidence." How do we welcome curiosity at work? We listen, and we ask inquisitive questions. We bring an open and learning mindset. We don't rush to certainty. The questions below stir curiosity.

Ask why. Ask what. Ask why again.

What fresh questions could be informative and helpful in this interaction or situation?

What is known and unknown about this situation? How can I bring curiosity to both the known and unknown factors? Are some of the known factors assumptions?

How could curiosity lead to a greater understanding—or an improved outcome—in this situation?

If you disagree with or don't understand the other, can you seek to understand before you seek to be understood?

Ask, tell me more. Come from a posture of curiosity first with certainty to follow.

If you are in what seems like a "sideways interaction," can you be curious as to what may be informing this interaction or reaction? Can your calm demeanor keep things neutral or facilitate calm in the other person? We don't need to know the cause of the sideways interaction; just that it may have nothing to do with you.

Grace is GOODWILL

In business, goodwill is treated as an intangible, saleable asset. It is assigned a real value often based on a company's reputation or relationships with its customers. Goodwill is also benevolence and generosity, a desire to do good with and for others. It is at the intersection of these two definitions that goodwill aligns with grace. In this vein, benevolence towards others, the relationships that we build, how we serve, and having a generous view of others are real assets.

Goodwill in action is to assume positive intent. It is most effective when we offer goodwill first or pay it forward. Peter Crone, known as The Mind Architect, takes this to the next level when he asks, "How generous can I be with my view of the people in my life"? He notes we judge others because we judge ourselves, but being critical of ourselves and others only limits us. I believe this bears repeating— judging others only limits ourselves.

Have you heard of the Pygmalion Effect? It proposes that we can facilitate positive intent by assuming it. This psychological phenomenon suggests that positive expectations lead to positive performance, and low or negative expectations can lead to low or negative performance, resulting in a self-fulfilling prophecy. In other words, people tend to perform up to the level that others expect of them. Thus, when you choose to believe people have positive intent, over time, you will most likely see their positive intent.

A close cousin to the Pygmalion Effect is the expression, "Whatever evidence you are looking for, you will find." If you are looking for people to be wrong, hard to handle, annoying, or less than, you will most likely find that evidence. If you are looking for evidence that people are fundamentally good, you will see many examples of people offering goodwill. Our thoughts and assumptions of others have significant power to influence our experiences. Nelson Mandela believes that just as pretending to be brave can lead to real acts of bravery, seeing the good in other people improves the chances that they will reveal their better selves. Goodwill may offer a genuine return on investment.

It is also true that we have all experienced negative people who act with a negative intent, consciously and unconsciously, and we cannot change this. But we can do our best not to let this interaction evoke a reaction in us. If we react in kind, we give this negativity oxygen and sustained life.

Much of our mainstream news and media, while informing, will leave us feeling unsettled. We may view things as "falling apart," and that the world is inherently unsafe and ungenerous. We hear of awful things happening, and we see people treat each other poorly. This infiltrates our minds and can inform how we see and treat others. We think we need to be defensive and protective to all the bad "out there," but this is largely untrue. According to Steven Pinker, a Professor of Psychology at Harvard University, "The basic problem is that journalism is a systematically misleading way to understand the world. News is about things that happen, not about things that don't happen. It's only by looking at data on the world as a whole that you get an accurate picture of the trends."

Goodwill is a mindset that filters for the good in others. It's the random acts of kindness that you will see if you are paying attention to what is happening around you day in and day out. Check out the Good News Network, a website that curates positive, brave, generous, and heartwarming news all around the globe. It is an awesome reminder that good things are always happening. It is true that we will encounter tough headlines and situations in our world, but I encourage you to balance this against the goodness that rarely gets reported.

I am writing this book in 2024, an election year and the year of the Paris Summer Olympics. As people express serious concerns over US and global politics and what feels like "the most divisive it has ever been," we are also hearing an increasing amount of incredible stories of sportsmanship at the Olympics. We saw US gymnasts Simone Biles and Jordan Chiles, who won silver and bronze, "bow down" on the podium to the Brazilian gold medal winner, Rebeca Andrade. Laotian sprinter Silina Pha Aphay stopped her preliminary sprinting heat to help her collapsed opponent. Brazilian handball player Tamires Araujo Frossard carried her opponent to the sidelines when an injury left her unable to get up on her own. And Japanese gymnast Daiki Hashimoto quieted the crowd to mitigate distractions for his Chinese competitor Zhang Boheng's final routine. All of this at the highest level of competition in the world.

But as we balance the yin and yang of life—and diverse interactions with others—we will at some point find ourselves in an uncomfortable or negative interaction with another. We will begin to feel defensive. Our emotions will get stirred. This is a very important deci-sion point. This is when we find ourselves in the space Viktor Frankl so eloquently describes as the "space between stimulus and response." Whether it is your boss or a colleague (or a friend or neighbor), this is a decision point where you can decide to pause, breathe, and stay neutral, assuming positive intent. Or you can let your emotions get stirred and pull you into any number of undesirable emotions, which may very well leave you with an incivility hangover.

We all say and do things that can be interpreted incor-rectly—sometimes, we just get the words or the deliv-ery wrong. This has happened to me countless times. When this happens, can we be generous in our view of others? Can we have grace for ourselves? Can we extend goodwill to others?

I created electronic messages called GraceRequests which make it easy to acknowledge or apologize when we didn't respond the way we would have liked to. A message that says, *To err is human or Ugh, can I get a do-over?* You simply sign your name and send it via email. No big conversation needs to take place (un-less you want that), but many of us bypass the simple acknowledgment to avoid an uncomfortable conversa-tion. GraceRequests are meant to make this acknowl-edgment easy, quick, and clean. They are available for download at my website www.graceintheworkplace. com.

How else can we offer goodwill? The following prompts may be helpful.

Ask directly, "In what ways can I support you in this situation?"

Assess if you were willing and able to assume positive intent when things didn't go right.

Remember that we are all imperfect and that you get it wrong some days, too.

Are you willing to respond with grace even though others seem to be temporarily lacking—or possibly devoid of it themselves?

Can you accept the tension, discomfort, and struggle of unwelcome emotions at work—and still give someone the benefit of the doubt or respond with unmerited generosity?

I invite us all to treat goodwill as the asset it is—a way to view people as full humans deserving of compassion, kindness, and curiosity.

Bringing It All Together

The attributes of compassion, kindness, curiosity, and goodwill all stand on their own, and at times are complementary. To illustrate this, I will share a client experience in which several attributes and tools were utilized. To set the scene, my client had several office locations, and two teams at different locations were experiencing tension, conflict, and stress due to differences in opinion on approach and communications in a client situation. As is often the case, these differences caused each office to "team up" and make their case to the other team as to why they were right. Each team was trying to convince the other that their approach was better versus exercising curiosity and listening first. The conflict between the two teams grew to be disruptive, caused delays in customer communication, and had risen to the leadership team level.

The leadership of this organization hired me to come in after the fact to debrief and decipher what had happened to avoid something like this happening in the future—in other words, they were curious as to what they could learn from this frustrating situation to avoid others like it in the future. As I facilitated this debrief, the framework of Grace in the Workplace seemed like a natural place from which to navigate this conversation.

Begin with Curiosity. I first asked the leadership to identify where both teams held common beliefs and objectives. Both teams were united and aligned around purpose, mission, and what a successful client outcome looked like. The differences presented themselves in their respective preferences around logistics, such as how and who carried this out.

I shared the spectrum of curiosity versus certainty and the spectrum of collaboration vs. control and how these visual, self-awareness tools can help open us up to other's ideas and perspectives.

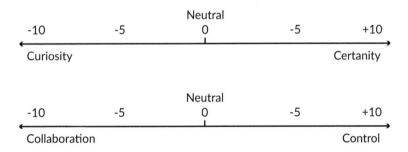

They are effective tools to serve as a backdrop for this conversation as well as a broad visual representation of where the two teams were primarily operating from. Individuals and teams can use these spectrums to self-assess or identify their number or position on each spectrum. In this case, both teams were operating at the high end of certainty and, therefore, wanted to "control" the logistics. This posture of leaning towards a closed mindset compromises our ability to listen and collaborate.

Integrating Curiosity & Compassion. After identifying where there was alignment, the next step was for both teams to take the opportunity to "seek to understand" the other before being understood. In this case, we were looking back; however, in future situations, this curiosity upfront can prove to be quite constructive. Using the spectrum of collaboration versus control sets the stage for the goal of collective collaboration versus figuring out which team will get control. In essence, it reminds them that they are all on the same team.

The exercise of seeking to understand works best when someone is assigned the role of facilitator. The facilitator selects one team to present first and gives them ample time and space to explain and support their position and/or recommendations. The other team is to remain open and curious, asking genuine questions as they arise or are appropriate. It is not the time to speak to or persuade the other team's position until the first time is given full and respectful consideration. When this is complete, the second team then gets this same opportunity and consideration. From here, the facilitator decides the smoothest way to gain consensus around the best path forward for the greater good of the organization or client. Consensus is rarely 100 percent agreement on each aspect of logistics, but in the process, each person was heard and participated in the overall design of the plan or solution.

Active listening from a stance of curiosity is one of the most effective things we can do to reduce conflict and find compromise. It may seem counterintuitive in our fast-paced work environments; however, slowing down to get clarity and alignment will create efficiency in the long run.

In summary, when differences like this emerge, individuals or teams can exercise a stance of compassion by identifying where they are aligned and actively and openly listening to one another. Identifying alignment on important aspects can soften our stance and open our minds to how the details play out. Conversely, if the alignment is in the details, start there and use this as common ground to negotiate around the bigger picture. Compassion is a pathway to other people's perspectives and ideas and where there may be alignment.

How Kindness Plays In. Kindness here is not about being "nice" and/or pacifying others. Kindness is being respectful to others and to the process. At work, we will invariably run into difficult conversations that we often think are about who is right and who is wrong, but they are more about differing opinions, perspectives, and motivations. At the managerial level, healthy tension and productive conflict are a part of our working lives. In this client situation, these co-workers retreated into their respective teams and then attached the problem to the "people" versus the issue or collaborating on logistics. This can be easy to do because people are what we see when we hear about the proposed logistics. However, kindness is extended and demonstrated by being mature and courteous in debating the issue or issues—in this case, logistics—not the person or people.

Kindness towards our co-workers—which is simply an in-the-moment choice we make over and over again—will amplify our ability to engage in and get comfortable with respectful debate to move the situation forward.

Goodwill. Bringing goodwill to a difficult situation is about trusting people and the process of how information and ideas unfold. From a mindset of assuming positive intent and allowing for a generous view of others, we can create an environment that facilitates collaboration. We can see awkward or difficult interactions as opportunities to enact self-awareness and benevolence. What can we learn? What can we give? How can we improve or move forward?

This practice of Grace in the Workplace is not perfect, nor will it be relevant in all situations. It is a simple framework that can be useful as we navigate the complexity of our interpersonal communications at work. In our final chapter, we'll explore the application of Grace in the Workplace and show you how to put these strategies into action.

Chapter 5

Application

Now that you are familiar with the practice of Grace in the Workplace, this chapter will focus more on how to bring this practice to life. I refer to this as information versus application. Step one is to acquire new information, and if you have made it this far, you have done that. Step two is the heavier lift of applying this practice in your day-to-day life, making it a verb versus a noun.

I created the practice of Grace in the Workplace first as an individual invitation for us to utilize these attributes, the factors that we *can control* to improve our interactions, our environments, and our relationships. I created it second as a movement, a community of people who want to opt in, to say yes to being the change we want to see in our workplaces. This movement is centered around people who intentionally choose to practice compassion, kindness, curiosity, and goodwill.

Often, when we opt into or adopt positive new actions or habits, we are excited and want to share them with others; I am no different. I encourage you to share the practice of Grace in the Workplace with anyone and everyone. But as you practice workplace grace, I encourage you to focus on yourself. This practice is an individual invitation because the only person we can control is ourselves. Yes, we can positively influence others *if and only if they are open to that*. However, the most effective way to influence others is by focusing on ourselves and our own reactions and behavior.

It can be easier to see workplace grace—or the lack thereof—through the actions of others because we simply don't see ourselves objectively. Are you familiar with fundamental attribution error? It is our tendency to falsely attribute the negative behavior of others to their character while we attribute our own negative behaviors to our environment. For example, if our colleague responds harshly to a request, we think they are a jerk (attributing this to their character), but when we respond harshly to a request, it was because they caught us at a bad time, or it seemed like a silly request (attributing it to external factors). We tend to let ourselves "off the hook" much easier than others so this practice works best if we all self-police ourselves (not others). You can observe, how would I have reacted? Do I respond like that at times? How do others feel after an interaction with me? We can use our observations to increase our own self-awareness.

With this in mind, a common question I get is, "What if I have a manager, boss, or co-worker who has little or no grace and/or does not treat me well?" I know this is happening day in and day out in our workplaces, and as mentioned earlier in this book, I am not qualified to speak on workplace bullying or harassment, so these words are not directed to those situations. But when we are speaking of incivility, I have two responses to share.

The first is that extending compassion, kindness, curiosity, and goodwill is easy when it's easy, and others are behaving in a way that aligns with our preferences. It really becomes grace when it isn't natural, when it calls on the "unmerited favor." It's grace when we can offer it despite how another is operating or behaving.

The second is that if you learn to practice grace in the workplace, you will strengthen your muscle of being the person you aspire to be more consistently, whatever that looks like for you. And this muscle of operating in your personal integrity will serve you well in all aspects of your life. It will bring you some peace and inner satisfaction amidst your current circumstances. And if you find it is best to move on to a new position or company, practicing grace and its side effect of personal integrity will be of benefit when interviewing for a new job and building new work relationships. Trust me, when you are operating in grace, you will only want more of it; it is compounding.

Seth Godin says in his book *Graceful*, "It doesn't pay to whine about your boss just like it doesn't pay to whine about gravity." This isn't to say that incivility isn't painful and unproductive; it's just that we don't have any ability to shift the actions of others—so let's stay focused on what we can shift.

Applying Grace in the Workplace – The Process of the Practice

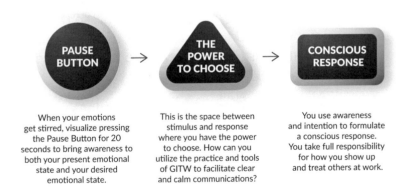

When your emotions get stirred, visualize pressing the Pause Button for 20 seconds to bring awareness to both your present emotional state and your desired emotional state.

This is the space between stimulus and response where you have the power to choose. How can you utilize the practice and tools of GITW to facilitate clear and calm communications?

You use awareness and intention to formulate a conscious response. You take full responsibility for how you show up and treat others at work.

This image is intended to capture the simplicity and essence of this practice. When this is new, and you are learning, being aware of the process and steps will be more important. As you integrate this into how you think—as you begin to experience the "transformation" of grace—it will require less thought.

The Pause Button. When you find yourself in an interaction that has gotten emotional (you are no longer calm, cool, or collected), the first step is to pause. Aim to pause for at least twenty seconds. Picture a metaphorical Grace Button like the one above—this is like the big red easy button from the Staples commercial that originally launched during the Superbowl in 2005. Picture yourself pushing the Grace Button, which grants you twenty full seconds; neuroscience has proven it takes just seventeen seconds to shift our mindset.

The Pause Button is a tool to capture what Viktor Frankl describes as the space "between stimulus and response." In that space is our POWER to choose our response." If we pause, we gain control to choose our response consciously, with intent. We can actively participate in the quality of the interaction—and, with that, the quality of the workplace environment and culture.

Once you have paused and shifted your mindset to neutral or an intentional response, move into the practice of Grace in the Workplace.

Choose Intentional Attributes. This is where we bring all the tools forward—or whichever ones are of value or relevant to the situation at hand—to ensure we act with intention. The "tools" in this stage of the process include 1) self-awareness, 2) agency or responsibility, 3) the practice and its attributes, and 4) the spectrums to assess self-awareness and stance. See below.

Awareness:

Am I operating and/or responding from a place of trust or from a place of threat?

Am I operating and responding as the person I aspire to be? Am I responding from my personal integrity?

Am I conscious that my behaviors and communications influence and impact the company culture?

Attributes:

Am I responding through a lens of compassion for others?

Am I coming from a place of kindness?

How could curiosity serve this interaction?

Can I offer benevolence and generosity?

Spectrums:

Am I in a place of certainty or curiosity?

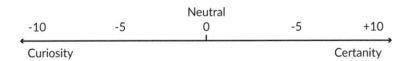

Am I trying to maintain control or to think/respond more collaboratively?

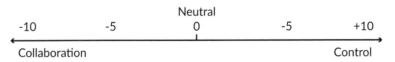

Am I in a stance of judgment or grace?

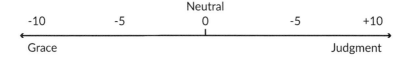

There are obvious situations when certainty, judgment, and control are the exact aspects that are needed, so you determine the relevancy and context of a situation and where these tools may apply. These spectrums can be most helpful when we are wading into unproductive or egoic certainty, control, and judgment.

I will share an example that is very personal to me and speaks to the spectrum of grace vs. judgment. Several years ago, I was upset with my older brother over an interaction during our Thanksgiving holiday that hurt my feelings. This was quite unusual for us as we were close siblings and rarely at odds with each other. But after this interaction, I became distant and short with him for several days. Somewhat unconsciously, I remained committed to my position that he had been unkind and was wrong. Over the holiday weekend, my brother made several attempts to repair the situation by trying to making me laugh, but I was having none of it.

Prior to this Thanksgiving holiday, my brother had been diagnosed with a neurodegenerative disorder called Multiple Systems Atrophy (MSA), which is similar to ALS in that your automatic and motor functions atrophy and ultimately shut down. There is no cure for MSA—it is scary and incredibly daunting. So at the time of this interaction, this tension I have created and committed to, I am clear that my brother is dying in a very formidable manner and that I don't have the luxury of time, of many Thanksgivings, to spend with him. Because I am aware of this, my position of anger and unforgiveness is confusing to me.

Within this same week, my brother's situation worsens when he gets news that his beloved dog needs to be put down due to invasive cancer. This came as a total shock in that his dog was eight years old and had seemed perfectly healthy up until about a month ago when he had noticed his dog slowing down. This beautiful, loving golden retriever was like a son, a brother, and a best friend to him, and now the vet is recommending swift action because his dog is experiencing significant discomfort.

Now, not only is my brother dying, but his cherished dog, who has brought him so much comfort and joy, is also going to die this very week. My heart is truly broken for my brother, and yet I am embarrassed to say that I remain pinned to my angry position. I think to myself, "Who am I right now, and why am I acting this way?"

I decided to call a close friend, hoping she could help me understand why I was behaving this way. Thankfully, she answered the phone, and I explained the situation to her. I remind both of us that I am someone who has committed to choosing grace, although I am crystal clear I have not yet chosen grace in this situation. And this is not a sideways interaction at work; this is a serious, heart-wrenching situation with someone I love dearly—and whom I will lose far sooner than I ever imagined.

As my friend and I talk through this, she helps me to recognize that I am still in judgment of my brother and how he behaved in our interaction over the holiday. And because I am standing in judgment, grace is almost inaccessible. I recognize that I cannot be in a position of judgment and access or choose grace; they are diametrically opposed. I must choose one over the other.

The second I realize this, I let go of all judgment and choose grace. It felt like a pressure gauge of judgment was released inside me, and grace came flooding into this open space with the greatest of ease. I called my brother immediately and was able to be there for him, to offer him compassion and support during this unexpected and difficult time. We both cried over the significant loss facing him and without talking about it, all the tension, all the negativity I had been holding on to was gone. This is the power of grace; it was another influential experience for me, one that I am definitely not proud of, yet the shift in perspective that it provided was palpable and again transformational.

When we choose judgment, consciously or unconsciously, we may block our ability to be compassionate, kind, or curious and extend goodwill. When we find ourselves determined to be certain or to be right, we may block our ability to be curious. Overtly or covertly trying to control things may impede our ability to be productive collaborators.

I recognize that these spectrums are not black and white and that we are most often operating in shades of gray (thus a spectrum). They are designed to offer us simple self-awareness and clarity as we interact and collaborate with others.

Conscious Response. In the example I just shared, understanding that my stance of judgment was preventing me from responding with grace snapped me right back into my personal integrity. After pausing to open our minds and evaluating which attributes or tools will help us align with our intention, the final step is to take conscious action. Conscious action is when we are fully aware of how we are behaving or responding. We don't allow our emotions to drive our response or behavior; we become present and respond with intention. My emotions were driving the judgment of my brother, and as I became aware, I was able to shift to a much more conscious and thoughtful response. It's simple but not easy. That is not to say that it is hard, but it does require conscious effort.

Have you ever heard the expression that "we pick our hard"? It is saying that it takes some effort, or "hard," to practice and embody grace in the workplace. But it is also hard when we respond in a way that we did not intend to, a way that creates some tension or discomfort for us and others. Both require effort; grace asks you to pick your effort on the front end for a cleaner response. Responding unconsciously may leave you with some hard residue on the back end. You get to pick your hard.

We are all responsible for the energy we bring to the room, to work, to all interactions, and collaborations. Observe others that you admire and those that you don't. What are they doing or not doing? How does this influence you to operate in your personal integrity?

The process of applying Grace in the Workplace is simply to 1) pause to bring awareness, 2) practice with intentional attributes and tools, and 3) formulate a conscious response. Everyone can learn it; everyone can practice it.

I mentioned earlier in this chapter that Grace in the Workplace is also a movement. A place where we can come together and build a community of people who value civility, who are intentional in how we treat others, and who are aware of how our actions contribute to well-being, productivity, and culture. If this practice resonates with you, I encourage you to visit www.graceintheworkplace.com to share your stories and join our "Gracist" community.

gracist
[grey-sist]

noun
1. A person who extends compassion, kindness curiosity, and goodwill.

Conclusion

Now that you are armed with an understanding of the practice of Grace in the Workplace, let's circle back to the situation or interaction you may have written down and apply Grace in the Workplace. If you didn't do this at the start of the book, see if an interaction has emerged as you read about the practice. It will help to have a real example as you apply the practice and tools.

I mentioned in Chapter 5 that the shift happens in the application. Unless we get to the actual application or use, we have only added to our already jam-packed minds. It makes me think of the quote from Harvard Biologist E.O Wilson, "We are drowning in information while starving for wisdom." Let's deploy this wisdom!

The exercise or application here is to consider in hindsight if the practice, the transformational wisdom, of Grace in the Workplace could have changed or improved the interaction or outcome. As you do this, you may want to reference the attributes, questions, and tools in Chapters 4 & 5 and assess how you could have contributed to improving this interaction or situation.

If I go back to the example that I shared in Chapter 3, where I was frustrated with my boss and applied any one of these attributes, I never get to my colleague's office. I don't interrupt her work, I spare myself from gossiping, and the negativity never gets oxygen. Each attribute on its own would have stopped me from venting to my co-worker. If I had applied compassion and put myself in his shoes, I would have recognized and understood the pressure he faced some days. Overall, he was an excellent person and a solid boss, and I certainly could have spoken to him directly from a place of respectful curiosity. It's interesting that compassion often leads us to curiosity and vice versa. Extending kindness or goodwill would simply have allowed him to be a less-than-ideal boss on the days he did not communicate according to my preferences. It is so clear and obvious in hindsight that I find myself incredibly humbled, and I have used this humility to increase my capacity to have uncomfortable or difficult conversations from a place of respect and curiosity.

Brené Brown says, "It is easier to create pain than to feel it." Sometimes, we pass pain on like a hot potato without even thinking about it or knowing it. But every time we avoid feeling discomfort or pain by creating it or passing it on, we place another ember on the "metaphorical fire." We become a part, a contributor to the problem we would change.

This all begins with us. Our individual choices day in and day out. Everyone can learn grace. Everyone can practice grace. It is a choice. If grace is not your thing, find other admirable attributes and practice them. Either way, I encourage you to be intentional in how you show up at work and in the world.

If you find yourself struggling with grace—or whatever admirable attributes you choose to practice— it may be the case that you can't give what you don't have. Practice grace, compassion, kindness, curiosity, goodwill, and civility with yourself first and foremost. As Tolstoy once said, "Everyone thinks of changing the world, but no one thinks of changing himself." Start at home. Start with yourself. Build your tolerance for uncomfortable emotions at work without having to react to them or give them oxygen.

Our workplace culture is not solely the responsibility of the leaders; it is the responsibility of all of us. Whether you work in an office, store, school, warehouse, church, or remotely, your actions and reactions contribute to culture every day.

My mission is to inspire Grace in the Workplace. This book, this practice, and my story are all a part of that. I also speak, facilitate workshops, and coach teams and individuals. You can learn more at graceintheworkplace.com.

May we all get it right far more often than we get it wrong. I'm rooting for all of us!

Conclusion

About the Author

Christy Clay is a business strategist, quick study, and inspired problem solver who facilitates real results. Raised in an entrepreneurial household, she began her career in commercial real estate and went on to own and operate four businesses in the recreation, hospitality, and consulting sectors. The focus of her work for the past fifteen years is helping organizations, teams, and individuals to work smarter versus harder as they navigate growth and change.

Christy serves as a facilitator for strategic planning and organizational effectiveness. Her philosophy on strategic planning is to Do Less Better, a balanced approach that focuses on planning, capacity, and implementation. Christy's insight and fortitude have helped many organizations to embrace change, improve culture, and drive performance. Her success stems from her ability to navigate clients through a variety of disciplines—

strategy, operational efficiency, issue resolution, revenue development, and strategic communications—to achieve tangible results.

Christy coaches leaders and professionals around mental fitness and increasing their capacity to lead and manage others well. Her unique combination of warmth and perseverance creates an environment for breakthroughs and mindset shifts. She facilitates clarity through a non-judgmental space to investigate challenges, limiting beliefs, and accentuate potential. Christy possesses a remarkable ability to guide her clients to self-discovery, revealing what is most important to feel alive, engaged, and successful.

Christy's work "in the field" inspired Grace in the Workplace, which teaches simple tools to reduce the complexity of workplace incivility and conflict. Seamlessly aligned with her focus on helping individuals, teams, and organizations to work smarter versus harder, Grace in the Workplace increases self-awareness and accountability around how we show up and treat others. The practice and tools illustrate our power as individuals to positively impact employee well-being, productivity, and profitability each day.

Christy holds a Bachelor of Science from Colorado State University and a Masters in Management from the College of St. Scholastica with a focus on Change Leadership. Originally from Minnesota, Christy now calls Colorado home. She enjoys time in the mountains hiking, skiing, and cycling, as well as reading and spending time around any campfire.

Learn more at www.graceintheworkplace.com

Book Sources

Centola, Damon. Change: How to Make Big Things Happen. New York: Little, Brown Spark., 2021.

Frankl, Viktor. Man's Search for Meaning. Blackstone Publishing, 1959.

Godin, Seth. Graceful: making a difference in a world that needs you. New Word City, Inc., 2010.

Keller, Gary, and Jay Papasan. The One Thing: The Surprisingly Simple Truth Behind Extraordinary Results. Bard Press, 2013.

McKeown, Greg. Essentialism: The Disciplined Pursuit of Less. New York, Crown Business, 2014.

Newport, Cal. Deep Work: Rules for Focused Success in a Distracted World. Piatkus Books, 2016.

Rhee, James. red helicopter—a parable for our times: lead change with kindness (plus a little math). HarperOne, 2024.

Rosenberg, Marshall. Nonviolent Communication: A Language of Life-Changing Tools for Healthy Relationships. PuddleDancer Press, 2015.

Weiss, Leah. How We Work: Live Your Purpose, Reclaim Your Sanity, and Embrace the Daily Grind. HarperCollins, 2018.

Internet Sources

Bill Benjamin, "How Empathy Created $250 Billion in Value for Microsoft, Last Eight Percent powered by IHHP, accessed October 15, 2024. https://www.ihhp.com/blog/2017/12/15/empathy-created-250-billion-market-value-microsoft/

Christine Porath and Christine Pearson, "The Price of Incivility," Harvard Business Review, accessed October 15, 2024. https://hbr.org/2013/01/the-price-of-incivility

Francesca Gino, "The Business Case for Curiosity," Harvard Business Review, accessed October 15, 2024. https://hbr.org/2018/09/the-business-case-for-curiosity

KPC Research, Weber Shandwick, "Civility in America 2013," accessed on October 15, 2024. https://webershandwick.com/uploads/news/files/Civility_in_America_2013_Exec_Summary.pdf

Lesley Kennedy, "12 times People Confronted a Crisis with Kindness", History Classics, accessed on October 15, 2024. https://www.history.com/news/crisis-kindness-pandemics-civil-war-911-attacks-hurricanes

Marc V., "10 Extraordinary Acts of Compassion in Wartime", LISTVERSE, accessed on October 15, 2024. https://listverse.com/2013/12/19/10-extraordinary-acts-of-compassion-in-wartime/

Oprah Winfrey, "Jeff Weiner: Leading with Compassion," Super Soul Sunday on OWN, accessed October 15, 2024. https://podcasts.apple.com/il/podcast/jeff-weiner-leading-with-compassion/id1264843400?i=1000419005587

Patricia Smokler Lewis and Ann Malecha, "The impact of workplace incivility on the work environment, manager skill, and productivity, NIH National Library of Medicine, accessed on October 15, 202. https://pubmed.ncbi.nlm.nih.gov/21157243/

Random Acts of Kindness Foundation, "The Science of Kindness," accessed October 15, 2024.

https://www.randomactsofkindness.org/the-science-of-kindness

Wikipedia, The Free Encyclopedia, accessed on October 15, 2024. https://en.wikipedia.org/wiki/Harriet_Tubman

Made in the USA
Thornton, CO
12/31/24 14:38:24